PEDIC'S DREAM

to Mary
and remembering Sam —
with best wishes.

PEDIC'S DREAM

Clive Watkins

Clive Watkins

August 2021

Common End

First published 2021 by Common End Press.

Cover image: "Cumberworth Green Man", a limewood carving by Chris Pye (Master Carvers Association), in the collection of the poet; colophon drawn by Ivan Frontani.

ISBN 978-1-5272-8973-4

Typeset and designed by Carnegie Publishing Ltd, Lancaster, LA1 4SL.

Printed and bound in Poland by Totem.

for Irene
for Noel, Zoë and Tim

Table of Contents

IV

V

Non è ancora provato che i morti
vogliano resuscitare.
A volte li sentiamo accanto a noi
perché questa è la loro eredità.
Non è gran cosa, un gesto una parola
eppure non spiega nulla
dire che sono scherzi della memoria.

Eugenio Montale

Ne never rest is in that place
That hit nys fild ful of tydynges,
Other loude, or of whisprynges,
And over alle the houses angles
Ys ful of rounynges and of jangles...

Geoffrey Chaucer

I

The Lid

This much, at least, is plain: it slips away like
    water spilling through fingers,
as elusive as a dream, although more real.
    Light from an October sun
setting behind tall trees is reflected off
    a near-by cottage-window
and strikes your face where you sit calmly writing,
    your gaze lifted to the east,
from which, in a short while, darkness will arrive.
    This is an analogy,
a way, perhaps, of avoiding the question.
    It's not hard to imagine
the oak tree locked in the acorn, its lofted
    full-leaved head alive with light
and air, but what of the tough cotyledon
    thrusting up through the soft mould,
or the fine house the ingenious carpenter
    will build from beams of green oak?
Indeed, size is not everything. The Zen monk
    walking step by step by step,
his mind fixed on the feel of the earth beneath
    his sandalled foot, is aware
of other things: wind rustling bamboo, water
    running over rocks. To reach
the path's customary end is not the point.
    These, too, are analogies,
mere evasions. Whatever it is, it is
    not like a Bach Partita,
whose conclusion sings on into silence, or
    a poem, say, at whose close
a lid snaps shut like the lid of a well-made
    box: open the box again
and the complex fragrance of perfected art
    escapes – but is never lost,
an ecstasy of surrender whenever
    you desire it. But surely

no act is complete in its kind, preserved in
      its own brief fire, an achieved
consummation? – The mischief of the stars, no
      matter their wattage, always
there, circling on high as if immutable.
      How can we keep our bearings,
you ask, in this delightful glitter-shimmer?
      (Was that click a lid closing?)

The Gallery

From the great gallery all the images have
        departed. They have left their ornate
frames and taken themselves off to another place
        in which at last they need no longer
dread the shrewd impertinence of being stared at
        by those who are not part of their world.
The elegant grande dame – wife or mistress of some
        fine seigneur: banker or lord – has walked
out through the door that stood ajar at the far end
        of her salon. In her delightful
wake the entire room has followed – tapestries, chairs,
        curtains, an ormolu clock. All that
remains is the grey gallery wall, the bare frame
        and, beside it, a sign that describes
the truant picture. From the hall the sculptures have
        absconded, and now, in an elsewhere
that is invisible, nymph and shepherd dally
        to their hearts' content, and, unconstrained
by whatever is thought of them, everyone – prince
        or peasant – resumes their endless life.
Yet still the visitors return, gather in groups
        around those missing masterpieces
to hear the learned guide expatiate on them.
        Rapt, they lift their eyes to each detail.
Such symbolism! Such eddies of emotion!
        And the artistry of hand and brush!
Magnificent! Cameras are aimed (no flash allowed);
        notebooks are filled; the experience
has occurred. Outside in the park a flock of birds
        (like a scurry of dead leaves) sweeps off
over the grass, above the granite plinths where once
        four stone lions lay in all their black
glamour silently roaring, swirls across the roof,
        falls back as leaves at the lake's edge.
Time for the gallery to close its high bronze doors.
        The streets are full. The streets are empty.

Portrait of a Boy with Imaginary Landscape

From where he sits in front of the high window
    he is unaware, it seems,
of what is pictured behind his head, the great
    absence that has occurred there.
His child's even gaze comprehends the room, where
    just now he has posed himself
on a straight chair – as the angle of his knees,
    his squared-off shoulders make clear.
The room is dark. He sits in a pool of light,
    which touches his pale forehead,
his slender hands. Those who dwell in this tall house –
    its seemly inhabited
clutter – are all known to him. The darkness draws
    nearer, as if it flowed up
from the shattered rocks that stretch out, behind him,
    beyond the glass, to a line
of indistinct blue far off: waves fall unseen
    on black sand; gulls cry unheard;
a brazen sun shines. On the stony plateau,
    encircled by high barbed-wire
white buildings stand. Of all who emerged at last
    from behind those walls, walking
away through scrub, soon lost to sight in that place
    of desolation, who has
kept true account? Meanwhile, in the quiet house,
    day advances. Reflected
in the glass behind him, a door stands open:
    he can tell without seeing
who is close by. Later, if the threatened rain
    holds off, he will run alone
out in the empty field with the homemade kite
    that rests by his knee. The wind
will shake its red fabric, ripple its long tail.

Unseen

Even in the smallest crowd – an intimate
    party, a gathering at the pub –
someone is always invisible, unseen
    by those who are happily caught up
in the chatter, light and heady, that flows back
    and forth among them, a statue's grace
and stillness glimpsed at the circle's edge; but shift
    the gaze, and there is nothing to see.
To compose from snatched half-glances the silent
    figure standing there? Dark eyes? A cloud
of sable hair, or the hair drawn tightly back?
    The mouth fixed a moment in a wry
smile as of one holding steady in her mind
    what she sees about her? – Suave fictions,
an opalescent dream to clothe an absence.
    When the party ends, and the farewells –
brisk air-kisses, the quick touch of hands – give way
    to the vacancy of traffic noise,
to silence, some there will be, the fortunate
    ones, who are for hours still haunted by
a ghost-memory that flutters at the brink
    of consciousness, in the soft margins
of sleep: a diffuse, unaccountable warmth,
    a sense that whatever it was they
denied in themselves – the ugly, the bright – had,
    for once in their lives, been truly seen.

Mirror Mirror

After the long corridors, the silent rooms,
     dust disturbed by the hem of her dress,
glimpses from the gallery of the palace
     gardens, long overgrown, her husband
gone, her lover vanished into a landscape
     of contest and avowal beyond
the perilous forest edge, she stands again
     before her glass knowing she must ask
once more the old question she can no longer
     remember. Her crimson dress drawn back
a little from the shoulders, her white neck clear,
     she stares at herself, and what she sees
behind that dead face is not the familiar
     bedchamber – the bed, its rich hangings,
the rugs spread on the stone floor – but rather that
     depthless dark painters choose as background
to a still-life: a vase of flowers, a jug
     of water, a brace of feathered game.
Her gaze locks on itself, the question lost – locks
     on itself till a quick draught of air
touches cheek and lip, her eyelids flicker, and
     the room clicks back into place – curtains,
bed, rugs once more brightly reflected. And now
     the tense murmuring begins again,
the ghost-voices whisper-singing mi-mi-mi,
     hands clutching at her knees, at the wide
skirts of her dress – mi-mi-mi – till she must turn
     aside from her own image and pass
once more out into the passageways, the thin
     voices lost in her hurrying tread.

Safe House

Here is what you must do. First,
find a safe address: a ground-floor bed-sit
    with a narrow alley-way
behind, a convenient first-floor flat
    with a private fire-escape,
a bright suburban semi (small garden
    in front, strip of tidy lawn
at the back) – somewhere everyone has been
    or is, which is why you will
think it safe. Go prepared for a lifetime.
    What you see from the window
will become the articles of your faith:
    smoke-drift from chimneys, the shine
of weather on blue Victorian slate.
    Everything you hear will breed
conviction: passage of cars, of buses,
    children's cries from the tight yards,
the slow conversion of time into things.
    And of course you will go out,
a necessary risk that yet declares
    the nature of your retreat.
You buy food, you walk in the park nearby,
    though you know you are never
invisible as you dreamed you might be –
    like the small birds that scatter
at your approach even before you have
    seen them, as you round the lake
to return at dusk past the shrubbery
    and the watch-keeper's green lodge
to the iron gates and the busy road.
    One morning a brisk rat-tat
will wake you early. Shifting the curtain
    you will know at last that those
who created all this have given word
    and the interrogation
is at hand. Even if you wish to, you
    cannot deny it longer.

The Heron

Lost in the ancient maze, he winds
about and about, searching for the one path
in that mesh of alleys and dead
ends beneath the sky's enclosing vault – hedges
too high to see over, glimpses
through iron railings into the next alley,
the next green corridor of dark.
How to escape? Gravel crunches underfoot.
Whichever way he turns, the paths
all look the same. Where they cross, pale statues stand,
their blank eyes steadfastly gazing,
emblems of spent passion in the gloomy hedge.
A heron lifts from the high wood,
blue-grey ghost, and spies him where he casts around.
Up and down he hastens, without
sense or direction, hoping chance will lead him
to the narrow gate he came through.
The silent heron, strange angel-bird, looks down.
Head in hands on a bench, the man
is weeping or laughing – she cannot tell which,
and then he is up, hurrying
once more along the endless shadowy paths.
Twilight. Beyond, among tall trees
the grim house stands, its uncurtained windows lit.

The Escape

An elegant syllogism
is as hard to deny as a blow.
So when he heard what they said
he stepped out of the door
and just walked away.

There were people everywhere,
but they saw nothing,
their conversation
the chink of stones
at the bottom of a dry well.

When he came to the bay,
a ship was just vanishing
round the headland,
leaving the gulls in entire
possession of the sea.

2.

By the time you walked away it was much too late.
    Already the thing had passed your lips
and entered into the body of the world, where
    soon it would brook no diminishment.
Long walks together among the dunes, the expanse
    of beach and sea stretching out vacant
to the horizon, will solve nothing, no matter
    how far you go, and the corridors
of light and dark the sinking sun makes in the woods –
    are they still haunted by red squirrels? –
the purifying reflections off the wet sand,
    will bring it all back to mind again.
But what should you do? Lock up the house and escape
    to another country? Canada?
Finland? Words clatter like stones dropped in a dry well –
    a drawn-out silence, then the sudden
rattle and skitter echoing up the black shaft,
    where you lean, waiting for an answer.
Too late. Crowds gather on street corners and huddle
    in the great hotels. Shouts of children
somewhere out of sight, in a bleak yard by the school
    perhaps, or a wide field near the wood,
are swept out of hearing. A fierce posse of gulls
    has found something sweet in the marram
grass to tear at, some dead thing partly mummified
    by harsh sunlight and the salty wind.
They break off from their feast a moment and fly up
    squawking. And what of the ruins, walls
still traceable beneath the turf, which remind you
    that this is not the only way things
might have been? But who is not culpable in some
    degree – so Logic demands – for where
they are now? At the harbour, consternation grows.
    The great get-away is being planned.
Round the point a white ship has just come into view.

Singing from the Same Sheet

for Irene

When I turn the page, the next is a blank, but you
    go on singing, driven by the syntax
of some inner harmony, some half-guessed-at pulse,
    although what you sing is pure invention.
But I, like a dancer who has stumbled, hurry
    and skip to catch up with the quick music.
Your private song continues, spills out through the French
    windows into the garden. The little
birds concealed in the bushes pay no attention,
    and the wind is not silenced in the leaves.
I alone, it seems, can hear you, as I struggle
    to keep up, my light tenor hopelessly
out of tune and time, your long improvisation
    rising and falling just within earshot.
And so we go on, I fearing your voice, so far
    ahead, must fade and die before mine can
reach it. I turn another page. It too is blank.
    And still the birds whistle in the quaking leaves.

The Notebook

It is in the end as if
the morning light streamed through him where he sits
    at the half-open window,
a black notebook resting on the oak desk
    beneath his hand, and what is
outside gleamed through his straight back, his watchful
    head, as though through gauze – the stand
of trees, the comfortable fall of ground,
    then hills rising up, a place
everyone had left, perhaps years ago,
    the houses vacant, the lanes
empty, a broad scoop of land across which
    no birds fly, and, far beyond,
the city where, once, fighting had occurred.
    Around him the bookshelves crowd,
the volumes neatly aligned, their bright spines
    visible through his body's
transparent frame, extensions of himself,
    his mortal nature flowing
out, a lucid intelligence, across
    their temporary order.
Yet in this moment they seem more solid
    than him, the words of others
subsisting in a space that should be his
    alone. The house is silent.
A breeze from the window lifts the curtain,
    riffling the leaves before him,
finding a fresh page. And look – he has gone.

II

Email with Blank Subject Line

My iMac pings to tell me I have mail.
    A single click will clear a trail
that leads through countless mega-servers back
        down a virtual cul-de-sac,
gate after gate, to where in the pool of light
    cast by your lamp you sat to write
whatever it was the arriving words made known.
        The merest overtone
of something barely heard? A shadowy hint
    almost too airy-fine for print?
Some thought turned edgeways on in your mind's eye
        which slipped away, a sly
ghost-creature vanishing without remark
        into the abstract echoing dark?
The subject-line is blank as if to speak
        of what remains oblique –
sunlight on water, not the stream itself,
    and not the sun; high on a shelf,
the volume safely archived, never read;
        the house untenanted
save by its noiseless past. Lacking that clue
    I only know it comes from you,
flying with feathered heels along the trail.
        I click to read your mail.

Beach Cinema

No need to dim the house-lights. Out in the bay
the sun goes down in a honey of orange flame,
and the stand of palm and eucalyptus turns
to a fret of rustling shadows. Spectral and pale,
we enter its frail illusion of enclosure –
beers from the Esky, the delicate chink of ice,
convivial whisperings, bright and intimate –
and join the others in our allotted place.

The sun goes down; darkness fulfils itself.
And now the bats take flight from the high trees,
hatched out in tumult from the leathern wings
in which all day they have swung in their airy camp –
a bladed clash of fronds, unearthly cries,
a rousing and a coming-forth by night
as the clamorous host leaves for the feeding ground.
We wait in the hush that follows their departure.

Eastward, the night descends like a sleek veil
on the three rivers, on the heights of Arnhem Land.
The sky's black crystal glimmers with alien stars.
Our conversations lapse. Beyond the trees
the tepid sea comes rustling up the beach,
darkness folding on darkness. We wait. At last
the projector beam flicks on, and the blank screen
opens into a world dazzling and cold.

Darwin, Australia

October Round-Up

for Tim

At first the sheep,
grey and white ghosts at graze
on the short turf, are deaf to the dogs
that drop down through the broken crags,
or the shepherd's whistles and cries
on the misty slope,

as right and left
he sends them, a double cast,
racing through heather along the fell –
boulder and beck and waterfall –
rounding to east and west
in a perfect lift.

The gathering flocks
straggle downhill and thread
past black tarns and rocky knolls,
winding through fretted bracken on trails
that interlace and braid,
a weave of tracks,

to the fell-gate –
the map their wanderings make,
being hefted to this upland grass,
where hoof-prints, dung and tags of fleece
caught upon thorns all mark
a habitat.

The dance plays out,
as custom says it should,
the dogs obedient to command,
instinct yoked to a human end,
varying at once their speed
or line to meet

each breakaway,
        quick feet, brown eyes alert,
ears pricked, teeth white as birch-wood peeled,
driving the flock to the sheepfold
        to jostle and mill and bleat
                at the cold sky.

        Safe in their pen
        they wait. The dogs are fed.
In the farmhouse kitchen, TV news;
rooks at roost in the tall trees;
        a tawny owl abroad;
                and the dance done.

Loughrigg

Bar Stool on a Tombolo

Who fetched this bar stool down to the white sand
    that joins the mainland to the Isle
with a curve of dazzling bone that ceaseless file,
the sea, has fashioned into a double strand,
      a causeway flanked by bays,
    a blade the constant wind inlays
with glints and flecks innumerably bright
        in the clear light?

What was it drew him here to sit and stare
    at the green water's lift and toss,
the fierce thrash where the tide-race cuts across?
Perhaps he came by night, in the crystal air
      scanning the stars that roll
    round the fixed axle of the Pole,
figures in a slow dance, keen points of fire
        that never tire.

From the grassy slope where the chapel ruins lie
    they are long gone who in that ground
concealed their hoard of silver, not to be found
till, winter and summer, twelve centuries had swept by
      the airy coves and cliffs –
    brooches wrought with beast-motifs,
neat punch-marks, interlace of arc and scroll
        on a feasting bowl.

The abandoned bar-stool is an empty sign
    set down within this limpid play
of absences by one who walked away
having watched and watched, as we do now, the shine
      that glosses the rocky ledge
    where seals bask at the island's edge,
terns scream and chatter, porpoises arrive,
        and race, and dive.

St Ninian's Isle, Shetland

Variations

Distance expands, over tilted rock,
over slubbed sand, crashes at your feet.
You confront dark waters.

They are not a form of music, you insist,
these unscored wallowings and roarings,
these endless variations heaving ashore.

Music was what, for fifty years, you made –
the unstilled silver pouring seaward,
scouring the pebbles, re-arranging silence –

and yet you hearken to their noise.
Going blind, you can no longer see
the hewn cloud of your mountain.

The wind abrades your ear,
beats at your gabardine,
and salt seeds on your tongue.

Reticent always, solitary now,
you will write no more,
the discs unplayed,

the numbered scores in their black files put by.
Your dog is deaf to such orderings
though the gulls' cries excite him, and the hissing sand.

He turns at the beach-end and runs
in a sudden flurry of barks to your patient feet.
His wet fur pushes at your knee.

The Sleepers

In the heart of the stone house they are singing, singing.
Their song pours through its warped bones like a tide,
rootless, companionable, seeps through knot-holes,
lifts by soot-shaft, by stairwell, between crippled boards,

leaking out from beneath the roof's iron-grey slates
into the still night. Its spilt warmth settles
among drifts of white phlox, damp privet,
sinking to earth in a field of drowsing cattle.

In the head of the house, the early sleepers lie,
furred in their slow breath. Some are abroad
already, their souls fluttering beyond the high
cloud, in moonshine, in star-shine, sharp and cold.

Planting the Fence Post

Soft rasp of cloud,
bog, bird-haunted upland:
day declares its bright distances,
miles of unaccommodating air.

The black shawl tight about her head,
she steps sideways down three
steps to the grooved stone of the yard.
Her dog barks furiously at nothing.

Dead leaves frosting into the grass,
a whistling at the edge of silence:
stone walls skewed,
briars choking the field-corner.

Stooping, he sinks the pit in its place,
the damp socket.
Balked by stone, the blade returns
through polished shaft and handle
through hand and arm
the ring of his downward thrust.
His shoulder jars.
He leans into the mute earth.

The crow maintains in the larch top
its posture of attention.

The Clock Repairer

Across the brown river's hurrying waters,
>   beyond the old burial ground and the bus bays –
>>   the one-up-one-down
chamber of stone
>   cut into the steep bank,
>>   the stone cell
where the fettler of warped chronometers,
>   arch-adjuster of tiny moving parts,
>>   skilled artificer of time,
second by second
>   corrects the delusive hours,
>>   the dark and the light.
The stone walls are lined with clocks –
>   bracket, long-case, cuckoo,
>>   clocks serious and comic ticktocking away,
and, behind glass, the watches.
>   Out of all of them
>>   only one runs true.
Which it is
>   he knows without thinking,
>>   who appears now
at the turn of the wooden stairs,
>   black boots mud-bespattered,
>>   stepping unsteadily down.
He settles at his bench,
>   a loupe in his right eye,
>>   his fine tools neatly racked beside him,
and lifts with accurate fingers
>   from an errant timepiece
>>   its intricate jewelled movement.
Not looking up, he talks,
>   the light ripple of his voice telling
>>   how, even at sixty,
still he will go out
>   across wind-swept uplands,
>>   in covert and close,

deer-hunting,
          having for a lifetime
                    practised in those wild places
the arts of stillness and concealment,
          the exact and difficult kill,
                    and gralloched his own beasts.
The work done,
          he drops the movement back in place
                    and, not glancing at his wall of dials,
sets the time right.
          Then, lifting his eyes,
                    I have throat cancer, he says.
In the winter dusk
          he will lock up his stone shop –
                    his cell of stone,
his chamber of careful time –
          and, leaving behind
                    bus bays, burial ground, rushing river,
head for home.
          He will climb up out of the valley
                    and, taking a short cut he knows,
enter the wood,
          watched by unseen eyes
                    hidden downwind,
to emerge minutes later
          at the moor edge:
                    frost upon heather and rock,
above him the sweep and flow of the stars,
          that glittering machine,
                    his stone cottage only a step away.

Hollowgate

Spell for a Cat

for Sappho, Chris and Jacqui

There was once
    (let it be told)
        a pretty little cat,
bold climber of curtains and shelves,
    furious racer along sofa-backs,
        frolicsome dancer round unwary feet,
and – *verbum sap.* –
    foe inveterate and deadly
        to whatsoever impertinent things
trail or flutter or droop –
    even the innocent weeping fig
        in its large pot near the window.
Will pierce with her needle teeth
    kindly outstretched fingers,
        nip at unguarded ankles
comfortably crossed,
    lazily rake with her claws,
        and rake and rake,
the good upholstery.
    The rattly cat-flap utters
        its three brief syllables
as in she comes
    from lurking and dallying
        among terraced monumental stones
high above the rippling beck –
    cat on the *qui vive*,
        praedal instincts stirred
by a feather, a leaf.
    Then silence treads upon silence
        as through the house
in her soft jaws she bears
    trophy-gifts,
        moist letters from the garden –

a bird, a mouse, a shrew –
    and over a shoulder where
        in a pool of lamplight
the woman sits peacefully reading
    drops them alive in her lap.
        Retreating to her snug cat-nest,
curls close about her wordless dream
    and sleeps.
        Her dream is this.
It is night in the wood.
    High in the topmost tree she sits,
        her breezy throne,
from that murmurous creel of air surveys
    valley, stream and hill,
        the gleam of distant cottages,
and below on the gravel path the man
    walking and walking.
        Her eyes burn silver and ice-blue.
With a single stroke of her paw
    she plucks and tears
        at the black page of the stars –
arcane figuration,
    black candescent flesh
        she eats and eats,
tiny glittering bones,
    splinters and zigzags of twiggy light,
        cast on the floor of the dark,
cypher, sign, faint patteran
    the man follows
        back to the stone house,
which is a house composed
    of words and time and words
        he and the woman –
by the starless wastes of the night,
    by the cold rush of the wind,
        by the water's flow –
share with a wise cat.

Magdale

III

The Small Kingdoms

1. The King's Mint

For fear of raiders, the mint removed,
the king's image huddling
behind earth-and-timber walls

on this tilted hill-top where cattle
crop the grass, from which due point of vantage
his whole domain lies under survey:

banditry, war-lords, the small kingdoms
defining the penetrable boundaries
of their own violent decay. Below,

on the distant A-road, cars flash back the light
in silence, and the cleansed plain
shines in the summer wind.

Cadbury Castle, Somerset

2. The Hostages

John Sellick (1610–1690) and John Bargrave (1610–1680)

In their fifty-second year
sent as legates to the Algerians to ransom
those taken for slaves by the Barbary pirates,

who had never binn beyond the seas,
nor could speak a word of their language and so
understood not their danger until it was over –

all one hundred and sixty two
bought back singly,
each from his owner:

those chained in cellars, those beaten,
ears straining in the dark, desperate to catch
the crackling static of a far-off world.

Wells Cathedral

3. Young Man with Didgeridoo

Its carved wooden throat
cradled in the crude up-ended
empty stone sarcophagus –

Roman, re-used *ca* AD 800 –
through which his cyclical breath
thrums, the echoes overlapping,

crowding with their pulse
cloister and aisle and the fluent
cells of shade beneath the cypresses,

where, at our approach,
a score of ducks
lifts into the metallic distances of flight.

Wells

Street Scene

Beneath the shadows of the arcade the flautist draws
about him into the silvery lift and lilt of gigue
and allemande a small crowd. The sound of strings
comes shimmering from the black speaker at his feet.
Late summer, early evening. His body bends and sways
as glittering phrases rise and fall, while passers-by,
strolling from river or square, pause to watch a girl –
seven years? eight? – dancing between the grey pillars
as if upon an uncurtained stage, turning and turning,
her eyes closed, in a solemn rhythmless pavane.

Nearby, the place of execution, calcined bone
and ash flung from the bridge; the stern mythologies
of bronze and stone – dire clash of arms, monstrous beheadings;
the narrow balcony where two dictators stood;
while, elsewhere, in a bar a silent TV loops
its bright inconstant images – a town in ruins,
talk shows, news from the high Arctic. The bar is empty.
The flautist plays. Some stay to listen; others walk by.
When the music ends, the girl-child dances on and on.
Her hands flutter in the dark; her small feet tap and glide.

Florence

At a Performance of *War Horse*

The house-lights dim, and we settle down at last,
floating now in a void, having lost that sense
    of what is near at hand and what far-
    off which, when we stepped from the bright bustle

of the street and entered the theatre's vault,
secured us in three dimensions for a while.
    What is revealed out in the humming
    dark is the lit circle where the dreadful

action will occur. Soon the deception has
begun. It begins with a low hiss of leaves,
    thin voices rising from the darkness
    as if from underground, signs in which we

believe at once: bleak landscape of mud, of fierce
atrocious noise, the poor flesh taking the sound
    like a heavy blow. Sudden flashes
    blaze into the head. Inexorably

on the plain move hinged contraptions – steel and wood
and leather – controlled by puppet-masters who,
    if we wish it so, remain hidden,
    the illusion of command maintained to

the longed-for, unconsoling end. Then in time's
sweet nick some who were lost are restored, not one
    undamaged: the articulation
    of a noble grief briefly sustained as

the house-lights dim up, and the applause declares
itself. Then the slow shuffle for coats and bags,
    three true dimensions reasserted
    in our awkward progress to the exit.

Outside, it is dusk. Yellow streetlights disclose
vast public buildings, dominant shafts of stone,
    cenotaph, portico, rotunda,
    the imperial statue on its column.

Liverpool Empire, November 2017

The Window

When the light flared and went out,
and the hot bulb crashed down
in uncountable splinters of glass,
grandfather was playing chess
with her two dark-haired sons,
while she in her accustomed chair
stitched and stitched and stitched.
Darkness fell like ash,
but no one moved or spoke.
Her needle paused in its flight
over folds of invisible cloth,
and the chessmen did not stir.

A few soft sounds –
the dry whisper of breath,
the click of the socket cooling,
snowflakes ticking the pane
that came huddling across white fields,
across beech woods barbed with ice,
to arrive at her darkened window.

How long till she stands up
and lights the waiting candle,
wakening into our dream?
She walks to the uncurtained glass,
and there are the cities of the world
filling the wide earth,
and the constant snow falling,
and behind her the empty room
where the game is not yet finished,
the linen unfulfilled.

A Singular Blaze

Lightning strikes,
and the tree breaks out
in hurrying flame,
a sudden Spring
that clads the storeys,
the stacked cells,
with a fierce bloom:
black pollen
caught on the updraught
fills the night.
In the hidden chambers,
in the passageways,
panic, escape.
There the unthought-of
creatures dwell,
the invisible ones
that creep or fly
in the corrugations,
in the branching dark,
disregarded.
How many are lost,
oxygen gone
in that singular blaze,
and turned to ash?
In the thoroughfares,
the inhabited places,
unseasonably
a fall of soot
seeds the earth
with carcinogens.
Crackling shadows,
bitter edges:
a white bird,
its feathers scorched,

goes clattering away
through heat and smoke
into free air
and slips out of mind.

14 June 2017

Pedic's Dream

"the brilliant contraptions spin like discarded coins" – David Selzer

For Pedic perhaps, at prayer in his cold hermit's cell,
Time was already coming to an end, the expected Kingdom
close at hand, and the Last Judgement – Hell's ice and fire,
Heaven's shining battlements and towers. Even here,
in this sequestered fold on the green edge of England,
he knows none will be spared. He survives ambiguously
in the name – naming the church, the motte, the ditch that runs
in gloom beneath the trees, and – faint trace in the grass –
the footings of an abandoned settlement. From the moist
bushes a flock of small birds skirrs away across
the uneven ground to feed on blown thistle-heads.

But who, in the strong lordship of coal, of oil, of gas,
and the great deniers, will be spared? It is late already.

In Pedic's dream, the angel carved above the door
centuries after his time takes flight, a mineral gleam
in the gathering dusk, miraculous stone wings aflutter,
as she summons into the middle air her diverse company –
serpent, warrior, horse; green man, musician, stag;
two lovers coupling, a smiling sheelagh-na-gig. They turn
and turn – rosary, wreath – above a land laid waste
by the fierce heat of day, by the fierce cold of night,
and vanish, while, in a distant sphere, strange new devices,
securely logged, some brighter in the evening sky
than the first star, maintain their silent watchful orbits.

Kilpeck, Herefordshire

Impossible Story

Along the banking, trapped among weeds and bramble,
      snagged in wintering hawthorn, rags
of polythene flap and tug in the fitful
      afternoon breeze, tassels and tags
the colour of dead skin, which crackle
      as if alive among branches Spring
will force into creamy blossom
      where, out of sight, the small birds will sing
and build their lovely precarious nests; and broadcast
      from cars and lorries and vans,
a scree of infertile rubbish undecaying,
      a barren litter of bottles and cans.
Before us the trunk road runs – above the river,
      above the Victorian railway-line that served,
once upon a time, the collieries: their leavings
      cluttered and fouled these valleys till history swerved
and a different age began. Beyond the hedgerows,
      brief hints of pastoral – a flock of sheep in a field,
a piebald horse, a red-brick house, a huddle
      of derelict barns barely concealed
by a line of leafless poplar.
      Our satnav's elegant protocols obey,
unwittingly, an imperial army's fiats
      and bring us at last – as this bitter day
hastens towards darkness
      and the January sun in a sudden blaze goes down –
to the flood-plain, the river-crossing
      and the orange street-lights of an untidy town.
And still our descent is marked by drifts of rubbish
      shrouding the muddy verge, choking the drains –
feathery strips of rubber, cartons and plastic –
      as though, when we have passed, just this remains:
a tough unkillable crop, a sour harvest,
      which, always in season, will not relent
but, surviving our casual dispensations,
      threatens to be our monument.

And what shall we find at journey's end? A garden,
     a house, and children's voices in bright
ascending rings telling, retelling
     impossible stories to the advancing night?

The Hunger of Erysichthon

When foolish Erysichthon took an axe
to the great oak of Ceres, and struck and struck
so that through bleeding wounds its spirit sighed
itself away, surely he knew no good
would come of it. A splintering crack, a stour
of twigs and leaves, the shrill light breaking in,
and lives that harboured in its folds all fled.
The lesser trees quivered in branch and root
fearful of wider clearances to come.
The goddess heard, and laid her curse on him –
that he be racked by Hunger, a malediction
hatched in the desolate regions of the earth:
no trees, no grassy meadows, those who dwell there
scratch from the barren soil a meagre life,
their children's bellies swollen, their legs like sticks.
Then black wings wrapped about him as he slept,
and a foul breath breathed in his gaping mouth.
Dreaming, he grinds his jaws, feeds upon air;
waking, consumes what the vast globe affords –
all night, all day the warehouse lights are lit –
until at last he fastens on himself,
gnawing and tearing with teeth keen as a dog's,
and makes a savage meal of his own flesh.

after Ovid, Metamorphoses 8

Legacy

And these, too, are ours – we who invented the steam-engine,
the petrol-engine, powered flight, but also vaccines,
the heart-bypass, the artificial hip, and have become
in this last age the quarrelsome ghosts of our own kind:

ice-melt, the seas rising, tempests, flooding, drought,
eco-death, urgent migrations to the temperate north.

The lizard's slow aureate blink. Its swift vanishing.

IV

Family History

John Watkins, Woodman (1804–1884)
Barnard Railton, Dee River Pilot (1764–1809)

Of the woodman and his boy, toiling this autumn day
in the steep woods below Llangattock, their breath a cloud
on the cold air, the thock and bright chink of the axe
sounding along the hillside, I am the unguessed-at offspring,
and the Dee pilot your own forgotten forebear, his cutter
sailing in a stiff blow close-hauled out of Parkgate
to meet the Dublin packet standing off Point of Ayr.

On census returns, in dusty parish registers,
the flowing copperplate, mute fragmentary annals,
blotted long since, from which to piece their far-off lives.
Yet when our courses crossed, what chronicler set down
that random first encounter? In the low sandstone wall
the wicket gate stood open, and overhead in light
and air the trees maintained their private conversations.

First summer of the Troubles, summer of the Moon Landing,
one night we sat and watched her rise at full, the bats
weaving beneath the boughs their swift recursive web.
Now, all around, this restless chatter and hum, rouning
and jangling, plain truth misprized as fiction, illusive images
of war, malfeasance, tempest, plague: shrill transmutations
of anger and desire in an endless gallery of echoes.

In this spinning world, we fashion out of ourselves nothing
that will endure. Such slight occasions: a sudden patter
of rain against the window, the leaves turning, October's
sweet rot underfoot. Their names and trades recorded,
at day's end the woodman and his boy came down
to the cottage at White Hill, and the pilot stepped ashore.
Salt-spray sharp on the lip. A lean fox skirting trees.

The Nail Makers

for Ellen Homer (1847–1917)
Daniel, 3 and 4

When cornet, sackbut, psaltery, flute and harp
sounded their various musics, where was Shadrach,
where was his son, Joseph, and Edward, his son,
and Ellen, Edward's daughter, all commanded
to bow and serve the image made of gold
Nebuchadnezzar had set up on the plain?
In the nail-shop their shadowy figures moved,
husband and wife and children bound in rags,
the windows open loops, the door flung wide.
From white-hot coals the smoke and flames arose:
the smell of iron heated, the bellows' roar,
the creak of pleated leather, the hammer's clink,
a sharp repeated strike for the nail-head,
and the tongs tossing the finished nail in the bin.
From a likely girl, at least four nails a minute.
In that unlit place not one who laboured so
escaped without hurt: their clothes, their very skin
took from the hearth its urgent tainted breath.
Silent across the yards of Rowley Regis
a caustic mantle of dust and ashes fell.

The profit flowed elsewhere, a dubious silt
skittering away in ha'pence, pence and shillings,
florins and half-crowns, incorruptible sovereigns –
fine clothes, fine shoes, an ease of gilded rooms,
while Shadrach, Joseph, Edward and their kind
were paid in copper tokens they could exchange
only for goods at the fogger's tommy shop.
It was hunger made them bow – but they rose up,
in 1842 marched upon Dudley.
The Riot Act was read. The yeomanry
bore down upon them with their sabres bared,
a bugle shrilling brightly for the charge:

the leaders taken, brought before the Assize,
found guilty, pleading starvation, and for this
only light sentences were meted out;
later, a dole of "bread and other food".

And Nebuchadnezzar? Aglitter with appetite,
he drops to his knees and falls to eating grass,
his body wet with dew, his hair transformed
to eagles' feathers, nails to the claws of birds.
Though humbled for a time, he is what he was.
The turbid river rolls. Hot oil, hot metals:
a harsh, peremptory music fills the air.

Black upon Rowley Regis and Old Hill,
upon Shadrach, Joseph, Edward and Ellen, there fell
a soft mantle of ashes, which laid down
in Greenland ice its dark indelible stain.

Rowley Regis

The Sty

Bare white legs astride,
he sits on top of the wall
above a concrete yard,
his alarmed gaze withheld
from what shuffles in that cell.
He is all of eight years old.

Deep in the low shed,
in the black stink of the cave,
something shifts, a heavy
displacement of the dark,
its slow weight thrust aside –
hot breath and heaving bulk.

It is 1953.
The August sun glosses
a litter of dung and straw.
The murderous Korean War
enters its endless truce.
Suez and Hungary

are still below the horizon,
but already Indo-China
has quickened into flames.
Turning, he makes out
a black clamour of rooks
at roost in the hedgerow elms.

Their imponderable speech,
a chorus of rough cries,
carries on the breeze
through the early evening air.
On what are they conferring?
(What stirs in the foul hutch?)

Twenty-five years on
the elms will all be felled,
stricken by disease,
but now in broken shade
a mare and two brown foals
shelter from the sun.

From the lawn beside the house
the voices of the grown-ups
rise in pattering talk,
a bright parenthesis
from which he has withdrawn,
ears cocked for the dark.

Quainton, Buckinghamshire

Song Thrush

for Frederick Watkins (1910–1960)

The eloquent absence of the song thrush from the garden
is filled for a moment by other childhood absences –
the whoosh and roar of a steam-train as it leaves one tunnel
deep in the cutting and vanishes into the next, a passage
between twin darknesses that rattles the window-sashes.
Is it here, or somewhere else, I stand watching in silence
as, before the mirror, you adjust your uniform to a tee,
your blue-water days done with despite the wavy rings
of gold circling your sleeve? Tarry smoke drifts
through the orchard trees and low across the unmown grass,
the forgotten graves, no more than sunken hollows now.
Perhaps you have just come back from taking lunch to your father
out in the fields where he has been laying a quickset hedge
or clearing a choked ditch, his labourer's task for the day.
What was it he said to you? You will barely live out the Fifties,
ragged decade of confusion and alarm. The smoke
thins. The hedgerows will be grubbed out, the tillage drained.
Filling the absence I hear an imaginary song thrush tink-
tink a snail, again and again, on its anvil stone.

Elm Hawthorn Yew

for Frederick Watkins (1910–1960)

Not the least whisper of your name in the tall ghostly elms,
felled decades ago, that sway and rustle in the hedgerow,
nor in the hawthorns, nor in the black shade of the yew,
which grows through its slow centuries near the church-door
until, as a boy, you enter there. And the pond on the Green
is filled in, and the broad field where the soldiers' encampment was
is just a field. Apprenticed in the echoing wards

of the destitute and sick, you never came back, claimed
in an evil time by the grievous disciplines of war.
Seven years at sea, and the long return: to a winter of hard-
packed snow, coal-fires and choking smog, a port-city
in ruins, and your old life. Where are you now? Earth's climate
swerves, brings things you cannot guess at: the tundra thawing,
forests on fire, the storms and floods of this cold June day.

Your ashes, cast on the city's garden of remembrance,
are remembered perhaps only by me. – A crowded silence,
a narrow door ajar: whose quiet voice is that
summoning the trees, their blessed airy presences,
the cool breath of their names rising through damp leaves?
Willow. Ash. Aspen. Hornbeam. Rowan. Lime.
Poplar. Hazel. Beech. Elm. Hawthorn. Yew.

Two Tree Island

for Evadna Yandell (1915–2009)

When all those years ago we drove out there,
you already in your eighties, both of us
fraught by a lifetime of odd stored-up things,
the precious or inconsequent debris
of choices made or missed, how could we know
that this invented island was just mudflats
three centuries back and not some ancient feature
time out of mind, the ditches, ponds and embankments
merely there to defend from the rolling Thames
some acres of thin pasture, thorn and scrub
(though where were the two trees?) which in later years
the Authorities would take for a landfill site,
decades of stinking rubbish ferried from London
and sunk in the wet earth, rejectamenta
the Thames even then was scouring away to expose
the layers of a past that was nothing to do with us
on that sunny afternoon as we sat in the car
with sandwiches and a thermos-flask of tea
watching the gulls, the redshank and the curlew,
and in the bushes at the edge of the scruffy car park
a volley of goldfinches, the two of us
holding on till the light was almost spent
while, westward, London simmered in its own dusk,
and the laden Thames swept onward to the sea?

Benny Goodman Plays "Poor Butterfly"

for Raymond Moss (1926–2015)

What's happening? Something is taking its course. – Samuel Beckett, Endgame

1. Afternoon Tea

On Mother's willow-pattern plates: the enclosed garden,
the bridge, the boat, the two birds. Here is his special cup.

Ten-years-old, he rests his head on his wife's shoulder.
Yesterday he returned from Cape Town, where he designed

for the celebrated heart-surgeon a brand-new clinic.
How tired he is. He sails tomorrow for New York.

2. Shadow-Boxing

Jab jab – one-two, one-two: bob and duck and weave.
Never been stopped. It's three a.m. The white streetlamp

floods the landing; the stairwell yawns. Afraid, she retreats
to the bedroom. Soon now the young constable will find him –

head down, stripped to the waist – seventy years away
in a cold hospital-courtyard, shadow-boxing by moonlight.

3. Timepiece

The view across the garden is wrong. He will not look.
Where is his watch? Beyond lies the sunlit estuary,

the big boats coming and going. It is 1945,
and the Benny Goodman Sextet plays "Poor Butterfly".

Tenderly she washes his face, combs his white hair.
Is it time to go, he asks? Something is taking its course.

Dead Ground

for Philip Watkins (1947–2016)

In the dead space behind the incinerator –
steel doors ajar, the urgent press of heat
from the opening, and a sour chemical smell –
a bulldozer had bulldozed into a pile
within the hospital's outer wall crushed brick
and splintered beams, a tump of dusty wreckage,
and cleared away what the May Blitz destroyed –
the German bombers, on yet another raid,
targeting perhaps the near-by Dunlop factory
or the railway-line. The hurtling bombs shrieked
through the moon-bright air and, missing their aim, hit
the hospital and a near-by terrace street.
Ten years on, and still the place was choked
by a ruin-mound, things maimed and foul and broken
dumped and forgotten there, a collapsing heap
on which as boys we ranged and rummaged, hopeful
of curious treasure among the crippled bed-frames,
crutches, chairs whose stuffing had bled out.
Is this how you would remember it, this sorry-
comic scene detached from our parents' war?
Tirelessly back and forth across the waste
two shadowy figures moved. *At the first blast*
he paused, crouching among the fallen rubble,
while overhead the helicopter throbbed,
the sun hidden in a swirl of dust and smoke.
At the second blast the hospital was struck.
From death's dark precinct you are gazing up
where the high wards once stood pitted with shrapnel.
For a moment our eyes meet. The grievous breath
of the incinerator lies heavy on the earth.

Foulness Island

for Vidanea Yandell

Not just the Seychelles, you say,
Tuvalu or the Maldives,
but here at the tip of Essex –
Foulness, whose windy acres,
won from the North Sea
eight centuries ago,
stand barely six feet
above the insidious waves.

Mudflat, salt-marsh, creek;
weather-boarded houses,
barns and derelict sheds,
the one pub long closed;
fields of yellow rape,
the dusky blue of borage.
But also, high fences,
watchtowers, cameras, gates,
on the foreshore spent munitions,
and everywhere the signs –
Official Secrets Act,
No Unauthorised Entry.
Through coils of barbed wire
cow-parsley springs,
a haze of greeny white.
Out on the glittering mud
the birds gather to feed:
sanderling, plover, duck –
and the avocet, quick-quick
on their stick-legs, that scythe
with elegant upturned bills
the inter-tidal pools.
Yet here in this watery place
they built the atom bomb
that in 1952,

a world away, would burst
in a storm of lethal ash,
an apocalypse of light.
The cold North Sea breaks
on the ancient shore-defences.
The sea-wall is breached,
repaired, is breached again.
Out on the Firing Range
mercury, arsenic, boron,
beryllium and lead
contaminate the earth.

Avocet, plover, duck.
You tell me how the birds
at each new detonation
fly up from the mud –
a flickering cloud of wings,
a ripple of weightless cries –
circle for a moment,
then drop once more to feed.

End of the Visit

Side by side at the foot of the drive they are waving
Goodbye, Goodbye, as the last car pulls away up the lane,
the grandchildren calling back from the rear window: Goodbye.
Behind them — stone of these moorland hills — their stone house,
and the lawn on which, from the dark laurels
to the evergreen's buoyant shimmering gold, the children
ran their giddy races: an afternoon unseasonably mild,
the April sky cloudless above this temporary place,
near-drought for weeks as the great river of the atmosphere
broke from its accustomed course. Dispersal, journeyings.
Round the wide arc of the bend the car
has already vanished homeward, drawing behind it
its diminishing wake of sound, its charged absence.

In this clipped unanchored scene there is no fixed point:
inexorable onrush into a future all scorch
and melt and break-down, an imperium of storms,
hastening out of a deep past this shadowy couple
waving from the verge entered only a lifetime ago
as a long war came howling to its ruinous end.
Soon the first stars will appear, locked in their vast circuits,
and a new moon will rise. A fuzzy image,
snapped quickly from the car, captures the two of them
moments before they turn back to the house.
The sun goes down behind the trees. A contrail glitters
in the early evening sky as a plane, flying at immense height,
travels steadily onwards into the north.

Guillemot

for Noel

"Better drowned than duffers if not duffers won't drown" – Arthur Ransome

When God commanded Noah to build the Ark,
he planned to destroy in a universal flood
his entire creation – all but the Patriarch,
his wife and children, and a breeding stock of beasts.
The remainder, drowned in a surge of water and mud,
their corpses scattered across the boundless wastes,
must suffer the justice of a vengeful God.
The Ark's design – its length and breadth and height,
gopher-wood sealed with pitch inside and out,
three decks, a window, a door set in the side,
and various rooms – was trim and trig and tight
to survive God's heaving seas, his keen spindrift,
while far below the busy cities died.
And so the tale unfolds: I am sure you know it –
the waters abating, the grounding on Ararat,
raven and dove and olive branch, and the rainbow,
bright token of God's eternal covenant.

But why are you building *your* boat? Perhaps you know
something we don't. That the River Dearne, an infant
flowing in peace down its quiet wooded valley,
threatens to breach its narrow banks and scale
three hundred feet of hill to where your house
looks out over roofs to the south side of the dale?
It's climate change, perhaps? We're paying the price
for centuries of burning fossil fuels?
But I think I know what really lies behind this,
not global warming and harmful greenhouse gases,
but something nearer home. Your project recalls
how three decades ago *we* built a boat,
father and son out in the cold garage,
and sailed her on the big lakes in the north.
But that was in a distant, different age.
God thought the earth was violent and corrupt,

but so it is today: famine and war;
beheadings, car-bombs, poisonings in the street;
the Twitter-storm, fake-news and the troll-bot;
Afghanistan, Idlib, Yemen, Myanmar.
(I think of my father cruising towards his forties
on the dangerous oceans of a war-torn world:
nothing about his boyhood could have foretold
convoys, torpedoes, and life in a foreign port.)

And so you construct your own boat, a Guillemot.
She's clinker-built, with a sliding-gunter rig,
okoumé marine-plywood, iroko, fir,
glued and screwed tight, all elegant and snug.
But you are tackling her solo, your engineer's skill
more than sufficient, I'm sure, for this tricky task –
measuring, cutting, steaming, always the risk
of a break or mistake that will send you back to the start.
Did Noah encounter such problems? Sawing and drilling
gopher-wood planks, pegging them fast with dowels,
did he have at his heart a dread of the Lord's eye
fixed on his careful hands, his accurate tools,
as, like you, he butted and fastened part to part?
In your intricate work, may nothing go awry.

I can see her now, spruce in her new varnish,
as, stepping neatly into her golden stern,
you launch her smoothly off from a rocky shore
high in the Pennine hills – a reservoir,
broad lake-in-the-sky caught in a shifting light:
peat moor, steep cloughs and a wide stone-built dam.
You keep your balance as the breeze carries you out –
a starboard tack, your left hand light on the helm
and the boat heeling. You are sailing across black waters
that ripple and cream and ply at her curved forefoot.
The wake runs out behind. From the stony beach
your wife watches as you turn on a beam-reach,
and gaily she gathers speed – as if to deny
she was ever a boat but is heading off into the sky.

Denby Dale

A View of Children Cycling

for Zoë

Everything glowed with a gleam... Thomas Hardy, "The Self-Unseeing"

Gripping tightly the soft black rubber grips
of the handlebar, I peer round over my shoulder,
but already you are a dozen yards behind,
out of breath and slowed to a rueful stand,
head on one side watching, as, freed from your hold,

I pedal unsteadily off up the empty street,
you still not far from our gate and growing smaller,
your right hand raised to shade your eyes as if
a sudden brightness blazoned the short day,
till, turning back, my bike gone, there I am

a lifetime later walking slowly between
neat drystone walls, while up ahead two children,
a girl and a boy, have paused in windy sunlight
at the lane-top, one careful toe on the ground
steadying themselves, before, with a quick wave

to mother, who strolls quite leisurely behind,
they push off once again through a field-gate
on the rough bridle-path that will lead them down,
bright helmets glimpsed above the boundary wall,
to the shadows of Stone Wood, and so out of sight.

Crosby 1952 / Shepley 2020

V

Invitation in a Season of Plague

for Chris and Jacqui Preddle
a' nostri luoghi in contrado – Boccaccio, Decameron

In this season of dazzling weather, come, dear friends,
and sit with us for a while in our green garden.
Sheltering at home, it is weeks since last we saw you.
Though creeping moss invades the lawn, and the paths
remain unswept, sunlight has honed the laurel,
whose tough leaves glitter as these vernal airs
riffle along the hedge; and the may tree,
its wicked tines forgotten, is drawn into flower.
We can offer you to whet your appetite
neither cheese nor olives, nor can we supply
quail in plum brandy, or pheasant, but must make do
with plain digestive biscuits, though it may be
dark chocolate ones are not to be despaired of;
and since you will come by car from your quiet valley,
we'll not have wine but cheer ourselves instead
with coffee or tea, chilled in a glass if you wish it.
Here on our hilltop far from town we'll sit
in the birch-trees' fluent shade – at a safe distance
as we are instructed – and tell ourselves fond tales
of those whom, north and south and east and west,
this pestilence has held us from so long.
And we'll discuss TV, what's good, what's bad,
our favourite films watched for the umpteenth time,
and the books we have been reading. (Wodehouse again?
Bleak Dostoevsky?) And I will undertake
not to recite my latest dithyramb,
so you will too. But, like a strand of wire,
sharp and unyielding-fine, through all our talk
the plague will twist and knot, and futile rage
at maladroit and scoundrel politicians
infect our meeting. At dusk, above the garden,
above vacant city streets, where traffic lights
still cycle through their changes, the panoptic moon,

rising at full, will gaze on tower-blocks,
on narrow terraces, care homes and B&Bs,
where those locked down are suffering and dying.
Come soon, for soon this unseasonable weather
from the hot south will end, and wind and rain
will keep us all indoors. The garden chairs
will be brought in, the sun-umbrella stowed,
and, standing at the window, we shall watch
the lofty birch-trees tug at their roots and thrash.

May 2020

Tonight's Poetry Reading Is Cancelled (1966)

for David Selzer

"evaditque celer ripam inremeabilis undae" – Aeneid 6.425

When at last we reached the venue, it was veiled in darkness –
    no one to meet us in the high-ceilinged hall,
a space charged with the memory of other voices.
    Were we early perhaps, or late? Was the day wrong?
Had we come to the wrong place? A mocking colloquy
    of ghosts whispered and muttered around us, deaf
to the Delphic satires, the measured ironies we had prepared,
    pale typescripts rustling in doubtful fingers, our lines
in that dismal room unread. Baffled, what else to do
    but journey back across the turbulent river?

On the other shore, our bus in the urban twilight climbed
    from the Pier Head and the granite chain of the Docks
past soot-stained Library and Museum to streets still scarred
    two decades on by the War – patches of waste ground
choked with rubble, rough clumps of ragwort, walls once scorched
    by hissing flames in which whole families perished:
unequal city, whose dark oceanic history,
    its deep occluded past, sang on beneath
the choruses that rose from dance-hall, bar and cellar,
    a bright amnesiac surge of wry defiance.

Now, in this older city, we who had not met
    these fifty years at last have met once more.
Ranged on your mantelpiece – your grandparents from Vienna,
    you as a young man. What private ghosts attend us?
To say they are mere tricks of memory explains nothing.
    Here in our altered world, where charlatans
and murderers prevail and the poor planet burns,
    we too shall soon be ghosts, and our fine words
no more than the indecipherable script half-hidden
    in the exotic textiles hanging on your wall.

Liverpool / Chester

Notes

First Epigraph: Eugenio Montale – from "Non è ancora provato che i morti" (*Quaderno di quattro anni*, 1977): "It has not yet been proved that the dead / wish to come back to life. / At times we feel them by our side / for this is their inheritance. It's not much – a gesture, a word, / and yet it explains nothing / to say that they are tricks of memory".

Second Epigraph: Geoffrey Chaucer, from *The House of Fame* (*ca.* 1379): "nor is there ever rest in that place, but it is filled with news, loud or whispered, and every corner of the house is full of murmurings and idle talk".

"Beach Cinema": Esky – Australian word for a portable drinks-cooler (originally a brand name).

"October Round-Up": For my son, Tim, my companion on the walk in 2015 during which these events occurred.

"Bar Stool on a Tombolo": A tombolo is a bar of shingle and sand joining an island to the mainland. It is thrown up by the motion of wind and waves. The tombolo at St Ninian's Isle in Shetland is the longest in the British Isles. The stones remaining from the small chapel on the island, just above the tombolo, date from the twelfth century, but the site has layers going back into the Neolithic and from the earliest times was evidently a significant place. The chapel was excavated in the late 1950s and again in 2000. In 1958, a small hoard of treasure, thought to date from about 800 AD, was discovered under a cross-marked slab in the early chapel layers. The island has been uninhabited since the nineteenth century.

"Spell for a Cat": The text of the poem encodes the names of its dedicatees: Sappho, Chris Preddle and (under her maiden name) Jacqui Dally.

"The Small Kingdoms": John Sellick was Archdeacon of Bath and Canon Residentiary of Wells Cathedral from 1661 until his death in 1690. His chief fame was his expedition in 1662 to buy back 162 English sailors captured in the Mediterranean and enslaved by the pirates of Algiers. Within six months, the enormous sum of £10,000 had been raised by public subscription, and Sellick and John Bargrave, Canon of Canterbury Cathedral, were dispatched by Charles II to redeem their countrymen. In Algiers, dressed in their clerical habits and wearing their hats, they had an audience with the King. They were able to obtain the release of all the captives, but only at the full cost of the £10,000. The phrases in italics are translated or adapted from Sellick's memorial stone, set in the floor of Wells Cathedral north of the Chancel ("ad Algerienses missus de captivis redimendis legatus"), and from a memoir written by John Bargrave.

"Street Scene": On 23 May 1498 the fanatical Dominican preacher Savonarola, with two associates, was hanged in the Piazza della Signoria. The bodies were immediately burned. Nearby is the Loggia dei Lanzi, an open arcade in which sculptures are displayed. On 9 May 1938 Hitler and Mussolini stood together on the small balcony of the Palazzo Vecchio overlooking the Piazza della Signoria to greet a vast throng of supporters below.

"A Singular Blaze": On 14 June 2017 a fire broke out in Grenfell Tower in Kensington, London, killing seventy-two residents. The plastic and aluminium cladding that had been added to the building was highly inflammable and caused the flames to spread with devasting speed.

"Pedic's Dream": David Selzer's poem, "New Heroes", from which the epigraph is taken, appears in his collection *Elsewhere* (1973). Kilpeck, a hamlet in Herefordshire on the Welsh border, derives its name from the Welsh Llandewi Kil Peddeg – i.e. Church of St David and Cell of Pedic. Pedic is an otherwise unknown early-Christian hermit. Kilpeck's tiny Norman church is noted for the richness and range of its stone carvings. The angel that figures in the poem is carved into the arch above the south doorway.

"Family History": John Watkins was my paternal great-great-grandfather. He lived in Monmouthshire and Glamorgan. Barnard Railton was my wife's five-times great-grandfather. He lived on the Wirral in Nelson's time. Parkgate lies on the Dee shore of the Wirral. In the eighteenth century it was an important port of departure for Dublin, both for paying passengers and official traffic. With the canalization of the Dee below Chester, which altered the channels in the estuary, and the increasing dominance of Liverpool, by the early nineteenth century Parkgate found itself bypassed. Point of Ayr is at the tip of the Welsh coast at the mouth of the Dee.

"The Nail Makers": Ellen Homer is my paternal great-grandmother. As a girl, she had worked as a nail-maker in the Black Country alongside her father – as had his father, and her grandfather, Shadrach Homer. During the nineteenth century the nail-making industry in the West Midlands operated through middlemen, called "foggers", to the detriment of the nailers themselves, who were paid with base-metal tokens they could redeem, at extortionate rates, for food and other goods only at the "tommy shop" owned by the fogger.

"Song Thrush" and "Elm Hawthorn Yew": For my father, who grew up in Quainton, a small village near Aylesbury in Buckinghamshire (the site also of "The Sty"). At the start of World War II, he stepped aside from his career in the hospital service, joined the R.N.V.R. and was made an officer. In 1946 he was awarded the O.B.E.

"Two Tree Island": For my mother, Evadna. This low-lying island in the Thames Estuary near Leigh-on-Sea is separated from the mainland by a narrow creek.

"Benny Goodman Plays 'Poor Butterfly'": Raymond Moss, husband of my aunt, Vidanea (see "Foulness Island"), was a distinguished architect specializing in hospital design. (He designed a clinic in Cape Town for the heart-transplant pioneer, Christiaan Barnard.) His parents had been Master and Matron of a Poor Law Institution, which was where he had spent much of his boyhood. Hence his interest in this field. "Poor Butterfly" was a ballad written in 1917. It drew on the story of Puccini's "Madama Butterfly" and later became a jazz standard, one frequently recorded by the clarinettist Benny Goodman, whom Ray, himself an amateur clarinettist, greatly admired.

"Dead Ground": For my brother, Philip. My brother and I grew up in the grounds of a large hospital in Liverpool.

"Foulness Island": For my aunt, Vidanea, who worked for many years at the Ministry of Defence establishment on Foulness Island. Foulness (Old English: bird-headland) is a low-lying island at the mouth of the Thames on the Essex side, fronting the North Sea. Since the 1850s parts of Foulness and its offshore sands have been used for testing artillery. In 1952 the first British atom bomb was assembled there.

"Guillemot": For my son, Noel. The epigraph is from Arthur Ransome's celebrated children's book *Swallows and Amazons*. Published in 1930, it is set, like several others in the series it initiated, in a reimagined English Lake District, the Lake in the story being a blend of Windermere and Coniston Water. The epigraph is the telegram Commander Walker, who is away at sea, sends his children holidaying beside the Lake, giving them permission to sail down to Wild Cat Island to camp. Apart from being a sea-bird, a Guillemot is a type of a clinker-built sailing dinghy.

"A View of Children Cycling": For my daughter, Zoë (whose two children are Teddy and Florence.)

"Invitation in a Season of Plague": Epigraph – "to our places in the country": Boccaccio's *Decameron* (written by 1353) tells how a group of seven women and three men took refuge at a villa outside Florence during an outbreak of plague in 1348 and entertained themselves by telling stories.

"Tonight's Poetry Reading Is Cancelled (1966)": Epigraph – "and he swiftly leaves behind him bank of that river across which none returns": Aeneas crossing the River Acheron into the Underworld. David Selzer and I became friends at the University of Liverpool in the early 1960s, a period when the city was culturally a lively place. (The Beatles' first single, "Love Me Do", was released in 1962.) Liverpool grew rich on the slave trade and the products of slavery. Liverpool residents still speak of "going over the water" when referring to crossing the Mersey to the Wirral, even though the heyday of the ferries is long past. Chester, where David has lived for most of his life, was established by the Romans and is, by several centuries, older than Liverpool.

Acknowledgements

"Mirror Mirror", in a slightly different form, won the 2018 Robert Graves Poetry Prize (Roehampton University / Wimbledon Bookfest).

"The Notebook", "Pedic's Dream" and "Song Thrush" appeared in *Pennine Platform* 87.

"October Round-Up" and "A View of Children Cycling" appeared in *Think Journal* (Western Colorado University, Spring 2021).

I am grateful to a number of poet-friends, who read some of these poems at an earlier stage, including Alicia Stallings, David Selzer, Julia Deakin, and particularly Chris Preddle, whose perceptive comments and advice have, as always, been invaluable.

Biographical Note

Clive Watkins was born in 1945. His collection, *Jigsaw*, a selection from thirty years of writing, appeared from Waywiser Press in 2003. *Little Blue Man* was published as a chapbook by Sea Biscuit Press in 2013 with photographs by Susan de Sola. In 2014 *Already the Flames* (Waywiser Press) was a *Times Literary Supplement* Book of the Year. In 2018 he won the Robert Graves Poetry Prize. He has read at venues in the U.K. – amongst others, for the Wordsworth Trust at Grasmere and at Oxford University – and in the U.S.A. and Greece. His critical writings encompass poets as diverse as Conrad Aiken, Wallace Stevens, Eugenio Montale, Edward Thomas, E. J. Scovell, Robert Mezey and Michael Longley. At his retirement he was the head teacher of a prominent high school whose origins lie in the Middle Ages.

Inscription

Soaped and soaked, one corner
prised up with a rusty blade,
the wall-paper peels back,
dropping in mottled ribbons to the floor.
A cold sun shadows you
through the uncurtained window,
moves round the walls,
its wintry light leaving no trace
on exposed plaster,
on continents of paper shiny with age.

Spilt water bleeds
into the soft green of your shirt.
Your arms and fingers ache.
You stand back for a moment, stretching,
roll from side to side your tired head
to work the stiffness out of shoulders and neck;
then, easier, set to once more,
soaping, peeling, scraping clean
the yellow bone of the plaster.
A surf of damp flakes settles round your feet,

and your arm droops,
the stripping knife grown heavy in your hand.
You step back once again and see
what close up to the wall you could not see:
the joke Latin names concealed
like a spell beneath the anaglypta –
MARCUS AEMILIA MCMLX – pale-blue letters
brushily inscribed a foot high
where tomorrow morning we shall hang
the bright vermilion wallpaper you chose.

January 1970